A Pocketful of Poems

A Pocketful of Poems

by

Craig Pugh

Published September 2021 by The Writing Dog LLC

ISBN 978-0-9701140-1-3

Printed and distributed by IngramSpark

Cover design by Wm. Craig Pugh

Table Of Contents

Dedication X

Ode To A Poet.. 1

He Had A Pocketful Of Poems 2

My Muse.. 4

Ethiopian Werka! Werka!.. 5

To My Sweetie In The Hospital.. 6

Old Stone Lion 8

Cupid's Apprentice 10

If I Could Just Finish This Freaking Poem........................ 11

Married To A Writer 12

Today's The Day.. 13

You Gotta Bark For Your Poem.. 14

Memories Of You... 15

Modern Poets 16

I Am Water To You 17

Thank You For Not Leaving Me 18

Cats And Wives.. 20

I'm All Yours Today 22

Love, What's With You? 23

You're Just A Heathen In My Temple Of Love 24

I Don't Know Where My Poems Come From........................ 26

You Lead With Peaches, But That's Not All 27

This Wretched Poem 28

Raising Poems... 30

A River Of Stars.. 32

What Would I Do Without You? 35

Saturday Morning Couples At The Market 36

My Cat 37

Do Lions Eat Poets? 38

Listen, Poem – You Have To Go 39

The Junkie Poet 40

Things Made Of Glass Sometimes Break 42

The Argument 44

Miss Muhondo, The Coffee Bean Flirt 45

Pie And Poetry 46

Kainamui Coffee From Kenya 49

Sex Slave 50

Lion And Turtle 51

My Barnyard Cat 54

Red Lion Amaryllis 55

Modern Poetry 56

Oh What Coffee! 58

Have You Seen My Brain Today? 59

Marriage SOS 60

A Poem I Wrote Is So Mad At Me 61

The Distance Between Stars 62

I Wish To Be A Bad Poet 64

The Author 66

Git On, Boy. You Ain't No Poet 68

The Dying Fall 70

Finding Myself By Getting Lost In You 72

I'm In Poetry Jail 74

Pluto And Persephone 76

Don't Eat Those Pomegranates, Persephone 77

Don't Ever Write A Poem 78

If I Were A Woman 81

My Poems 82

The Cat And I 83

The Break Up 84

Growing Poets 86

Cat Lovers Visit The Dog Park 88

Senior Center Poetry Class 90

Poetry Infestation 92

I Want You To Be Happy 94

I Got A Deal For You 96

The Weary Poet 97

About The Author 98

Dedication

When I graduated from high school 51 years ago, my parents gave me a slim volume of poetry as a gift in which my father wrote:
"With all the love and pride parents can feel for a fine son."

I now give these words back to my Dad, with all the love and pride a son can feel for a fine father. Dad, this book of poems is for you.

For my Father, Colonel (Ret.) William M. Pugh: Last of the iron bombers, a fighter pilot extraordinaire, Wild Weasel, Thud Driver and SAM-Slayer. Fire in the air and thunder on the ground coming in hot and heavy to lay it down.

And for you reading this now. May my words find you with lucky
dice in your pocket and the odds in your favor.

We both know life's a game of chance with
winners and losers, and we're a pair of dice
thrown by drunken gods playing the odds.
We hit the table hoping for snake eyes
and bust out when the toss turns otherwise.

We're survivors, then, you and I who try
and keep our faces to the light. Clutching faith
and what's left of broken hearts and loves,
we hold on, praying for moments of grace.

from: I Got A Deal for You, pg. 96

Ode To A Poet

Poet, you let your passions get the best of you.
It's understatement to say you burn too hot.
You give every experience all you got although
it's not necessary to carry on that way each day.

You do it anyway. You seek to crush the universe
with your fist yet only end up breaking your wrist.
You insist on holding all the emotions in your heart
where they spin around, tearing and ripping it apart.

He Had A Pocketful Of Poems

Thin and with a full head of wavy blond hair
he walked around downtown each year until
he got old and his golden mane turned grey.
Then I watched him walk some more as I did
from my condo perch overlooking Tenth Street.

I kept seeing him in the rain, the cold and heat.
One winter I watched him pitch headfirst into
the chain-link fence across the street as he slipped
leaping a snowbank trying to reach the sidewalk.

Lucky he wore a stocking cap that day or he would have
gashed his forehead in a bad way. Instead, he rose up
and kept going, holding both hands to his head. Friend
it was minus ten degrees with a wind chill of zero so
I suppose his blood would have froze, not flowed.

A piece of paper slipped out his back pocket and
not seeing it, he stumbled on in the sleet. I ran down
to retrieve it out of curiosity and saw it was a poem
about a daughter who wouldn't speak to her father.

Once I saw him standing under the William Street Bridge
waiting for the rain to stop, and certainly as I've driven
to work in the morning I've spotted him out hiking about
hands in his pockets, or else waiting at some crosswalk.

And one time I saw him kneeling down in front of
that old piece of concrete in the parking lot down on
Fourteenth Street, the one with a lion's face carved on it
and it looked to me like he was crying. I don't know what
he saw but I'll bet you a dollar he got a poem out of it.

Then one night I was coming home late, driving under
the Thirteenth Street bridge, an ugly piece of shit even in
daylight: all scary and dark with trains thundering overhead.

And – incredibly -- he strode under it, waving his arms
punching the air like a boxer, screaming at the top of
his voice: *Come on you sons of bitches! I'll kill you all*!

Can you imagine what demons he kept in his head?
He walked among homeless people, violent folks and
crazy ones, too. One morning at four a.m. I saw him
running from three drunks chasing him for his coat.

Good luck to them! That old boy had the legs of a goat
that served him well as he walked off all that energy
inside him that kept trying to blow out in explosions.
Head down, looking like he'd just lost his best friend
he walked, everything weighing so heavy upon him.

He seemed to die a thousand deaths with every breath
he took trudging all those years in all types of weather
with emotional riots exploding inside him. I once read
a poem of his about jumping off the Bob Kerry Bridge
and realized he probably walked around thinking about it.

Which is weird, because one day he flat-out disappeared.
Man, I hope he's somewhere really nice, anywhere but here in
this prairie town where nothing ever goes or comes around.
And certainly not down on the bottom of the Missouri River.

I watched him walk year after year in rain and sleet and
summer heat and freezing winter cold. What stories
he must have told. What a character he must have been.
A real contradiction: strong yet weak; tough yet broken.
A wisp of a man who walked around with a pocketful of poems.

My Muse

My muse is like an impatient man.
She likes having her way with me
whenever she can. Why, the other day
I was driving home from the store and
almost pulled over three times or more!

Why's that? A poem was coming through.
Damn, girl. Can't you wait? I'm driving.

I park at the curb, dash to the house.
Neighbors say "Gotta pee?" No, you see
it's just my muse having her way with me.

I have to run inside and write down the lines
before something jars them from my mind.

You see, she demands to be taken care of first.
Isn't this just like a man? I can see her smiling now,
beguiling and somewhat unforgiving. Wrapping me
around her little finger with a pink satin ribbon.

Ethiopian Werka! Werka!

Werka Werka coffee from Ethiopia, I like to say
your name twice because it's fun like a pun and
I'm a huge coffee fool, which is why it's so cool
I ran into you coming off such a torrid affair with
Miss Kanake from Kenya. What can I say?

She threw herself on me with tangerines and not sugar
but *raw* sugar, and not fruit but *passion* fruit.
Wow. Tangerines topped with passion and sugar!

So of course I thought I took some LSD and got myself
inside a coffee dream in some hallucinatory capacity.
Wouldn't you? Anyway, Miss Kanake . . . head spinner!

Such a fool I made of myself with that tangerine tart.
Uptown, downtown and in the park. Sure, people stared
and talked. Did I care? Hell no. Not with her in my cup!

I think you can see how badly I need a new coffee now.
One I can drink like a grownup and not blowup. A real
chamber-of-commerce coffee with body and character.
Kanake had lots of body; she just didn't have any character.

Which made me so glad to meet you, Werka Werka,
rounding the corner with your hibiscus, peaches and not tea
but *black* tea, hinting at something dark and naughty. I'm in!
Okay -- just kidding. Truth be told, I've settled down.
No more passion fruit and raw sugar for this coffee clown.

That's why it was so great, Werka Werka, that with my very
first sip of you I knew Miss Kanake and I were through. So yeah,
Ethiopian Werka Werka -- I think you're gonna worka! worka!

To My Sweetie In The Hospital

Honey, I know you had to go into the hospital and that was
a good thing because you were really suffering from your
cellulitis infection, burning with fever and hot to the touch.

I hurt for you so much! And though I'm sad you're gone I'm
glad you're propped up in a bed instead of home doing laundry
or dishes and listening to me bitch about my latest quandary or
fight with the world. If you were here I might also be yelling at
you to fix the printer. It's always on the fritz. You know what?
I'm willing to admit the truth. If anyone needed a rest, you do.

So I'm happy for you and don't worry: things are fine; well, most of
the time. I know you're anxious for a report, so I'll keep it short.
First of all, the rent is late. Sure, it was the end of the month but I
forgot the date what with all the phone calls and texting and driving
back and forth to the hospital I evidently lost track of the time.

Then the landlord called and said he's appalled at our negligence
and now will add a fifty-dollar late fee to the rent I haven't sent yet
because I can't find the checkbook. Do you know where the heck it is?
Then there's the mail key. Have you seen it? It's been days now

and I can't open the box. All of this feels weirdly Shakespearean as if
there's a *pox upon our house.* And I feel like such a louse. American
Express is really distressed I haven't made a payment while VISA and
MasterCard are griping hard that I should send a few dollars in.

So is the dentist. And then, just last night I fixed a toddy (Only one,
mind you, solely for the body. Okay, maybe two.) when the cat
nipped at my shin and drew blood. He ran away this morning.

Honestly, it was an accident. I opened the door to take out the trash
and off he went in a mad dash and at a high sprint. It's inaccurate to
say his rear end bears my shoeprint. He's not gone far. Just a minute
ago I saw him jumping from the hood of a car to the top of the
parking lot dumpster. He was looking quite spry. He poked around
for a bit, then came up chewing on what looked like a chicken thigh.

Oh, and we're out of food. I need to get some but you know how
much I hate shopping. Perhaps you can do that when you come
home. You are coming home, aren't you? You can see how I'm
getting by just fine. Forget the fact that I sit on my bed and cry at
night because nothing in my life's working. I'm okay. But wait.
I smell smoke. Honey, let me get back to you. Something's burning!

Old Stone Lion

Stone lion, it's always good to see you.
No matter the season or time of day
I enjoy gazing at your regal bearing
perched atop the old concrete pillar
in this bleak and abandoned parking lot.

You sit alone and I, your kindred spirit,
walk alone, which is why I often stop
to see if you have anything to say.

I believe you must, for I look at you
in all your kingly glory and think:
I'll bet that fellow has a fine story!

Your brow is scored with furrowed marks
I'm sure you earned from years of wisdom.
I beg you therefore please share your vision
of how to be a regal beast ruling a kingdom.

Yet for all your splendor I sense an inhibition.
Is there something you forgot or a bad thought
that got caught up in one of your dreadlocks?

I'm sure in your day you were quite dashing
but now I see you lack some good old-fashioned
lion passion. Shouldn't you be out romping
and roaring all over the African savanna
humping lionesses and tearing into hyenas
then ending such pleasures with royal snoozes?

That's the path I would choose if I were a lion
like you. Wait . . . don't tell me. Those days.
They're over for you, aren't they? Oh my gosh!

You were caught up in a palace coup and
chased off by a younger version of you,
your days of roaring decidedly through.
Now I know what makes you blue.
You're a deposed lion, aren't you?

Friend Leo, we can't break bread or eat.
Can't taste the grape and toast to fate
with quaffs of wine. You're a stone lion.
You can't eat. Don't worry. I'll sit and we
can share stories in a mental feast instead.

And if it's tears you want to shed, we can
get to crying; for I, too, am a deposed lion.

But you and I will soon be dying and lying
in our graves. So let's enjoy each other's
company underneath this shade today.

Cupid's Apprentice

Yes, I'm Cupid's apprentice. But
he's the lucky one. He got love.

Therefore, with tousled locks
of golden hair he beats his wings
for maidens fair, fluttering o'er
woodland paths divine where
lovers walk with hands entwined.

The Queen of Hearts then sets him right.
She guides his arrows in certain flight.
Then all you singles now are wed,
lying as you are in Cupid's bed.

I didn't get love. I got words: nouns, verbs,
pronouns and adjectives. Relative clauses.

Not for me a shady grove, flowering garden
or courting bench. I was handed a writing tablet
and ordered to fill it with words, inch-by-inch.

So, with jumbled thoughts in fraught despair
I beat my pen for phrases fair. Down the page
and then back up, tasting rejection's bitter cup.

I pray Mercury doth alight to make my words
steady and bright so I, a stranger, could taste
fame and be a man who's mastered his game.

Tis true: The son of Venus never misses.
Yet I wait for Mercury to blow me kisses.

If I Could Just Finish This Freaking Poem

Honey, I know I've been out of sorts lately and
that's putting it mildly. I can't see straight and
my brain spins around like blender blades on hi.

I can't sleep, won't eat and start fights. Nothing
comes out right. I even lost my sexual appetite.
I need a magic genie to grant me just one wish.

If that could occur all I would ask for are the words
to finish this freaking poem. Without this poem
my life's all ruined. There won't be any beer
a-brewing or chickens worth roasting or chewing.

Our dog, intuitive beast, knows better than to fetch
his leash. He doesn't dare bark nor dream he'll get
a walk in the park today. Sorry. No way, Jose.

Neither will the cat sit on my lap nor you speak to me
ever since this poem stretched me out on its rack.
I work on it all day, only to end up with a sore back.

As for my poetically poor meter and beats, good Lord!
They're all crooked and cracked and hobbling along
on broken feet. Iambic or trochaic? Who knows? Not me!

I'm tearing my hair out, cursing the gods, the moon
and the stars. And I confess to putting you in a swoon
or two while I tried getting this poem to come through.

I've unfortunately gone this crazy many times before
and I'm sure we both know I'll regain my mind and be
perfectly fine just as soon as I finish this freaking poem.

For the moment, however, I apologize that nothing I write
works and it appears that poetry has turned me into a jerk.

Married To A Writer

Honey, I know I don't spend as much time
with you as I should. We've been married
so long I just assume everything's all good.

Like today, for example. I hope you're fine.
And me? I'm okay. But it's the same old deal.
I can't stop writing. So I'm happy you're out
shopping and will return to cook a meal.

And by all means, don't forget to text
when you get here, honk if you're horny
and cry out if you need some help.

Today's The Day

Today's the day I'm going to nail.
Every card I toss will go in the pail.
The dice will come up snake-eyes.
I'm running the race for first prize.

I'm going to make the flame roar
and soar into the stratosphere.
Put Earth in my rearview mirror.
Win at the track when I come back
then get the fire in my veins before
I grab the reins and drive the train.

I'll take the offer I can't refuse, beat
the odds, get lucky at cards and place
the bet that's impossible to lose.

I'll get the check in the mail and on
my way I'm pulling the tiger's tail.
If he wails I'll give him a smack because
Dame Fortune's got my back. All I see
is mine to have. Powerball is up for grabs.

It's all smiles from here. Movie stars
fast cars, pretty girls and ice-cold beer.
Good luck draws ever nearer all because
today's the day I'm going to nail.

You Gotta Bark For Your Poem

I was working on a poem this week
and it was so hard I had to sneak up
on it because I knew if I got too close
to it I'd be staring over a cliff and down
into a chasm of emotional despair
so great I would have jumped in.

So I was crawling up to this poem
on my hands and knees like a soldier
in a minefield, going forward slowly
sliding my bayonet into the ground
each time with a prayer while trying
not to trigger a depression detonator.

Devil come along, looked at me and said:
Son, why you crawling around on all fours
like a low-down dog? I explained it for him.

He said that being the case, would I bark like
one for him? I replied: *Bark like a dog for you?*
I should think not thou prince of darkness
and smelly old warlock. Get off my porch.
I bark for no man and certainly not Satan.

The Devil laughed and said *What if I gave*
you a poem of great delight? The best one
you'll ever write? One that caused fame
to light upon your brow. Would that get
you down on all four barking for me now?

I thought a minute and scratched my chin
before finally looking up at him and saying:
Ok, Satan. What kind of dog you got in mind?
Shih Tzu, Pit Bull, Pekinese or Pug? Arf! Arf!

Memories Of You

My mind is a cat at three a.m. waiting
for me to wake up so the fun can begin.

I leave the bed to pee and he's all in, all
this for that, all tit for tat and bouncy
bouncy, bouncy. Then he thinks he sees
a rat and goes pouncy, pouncy, pouncy.

My mind of a cat brings me many things:
balled-up gum wrappers, pieces of string
rodent skulls and broken wings along with
birds and bits of feathers all of which incur
my displeasure, but none more than you.

I like my cat. He's my best friend.
But I get angry when he brings you in.
Yours is the biggest mess to clean up.
I can't mop your memories off the floor.
Neither can I scrub them from the door.

I ask my mind of a cat to bring me things
more appropriate for a feline friend other
than memories of you that make me blue.
But he just flashes me his little kitten grin.
Then runs back out and brings you in again.

Modern Poets

I don't mean to be such a prude but
don't you think it's rude to talk about
genitalia in mixed company? I swear

these modern poets can't keep sex out
of their rhyme. They write about it lots
and all of the time. I figure they must be

quite an incestuous bunch who think
the best poetry comes out of a hot crotch.
(Sorry by the way to bring that image up.)

So go ahead: call me old-fashioned if you wish.
I for one won't be dashing off verses with such
images. I'm averse to dirty-minded businesses.
I don't hang out at strip joints stuffing dollar bills
in thongs or cruise the internet craving for porn.
Nor do I read poets who can't keep their pants on.

That's just Point A. Point B is this if you haven't
noticed: you can't understand modern poets.
So how do get satisfaction from scribblers
who toil in smoke and fog and abstractions?
Tell me what's wrong with making sense!

Please don't make me search for meaning.
Honestly, does anyone have time nowadays
to figure out pieces of head-scratching rhyme?
No! Why, it's indefensible to be nonsensical.

So there you have it. I gave you Point A and
Point B, too. That's enough proof to show you
how modern poets are perverts and miscreants
who can't for their own sakes make any sense.

I Am Water To You

I was a water molecule first, then lived in a cloud
before I fell on you. I remember your tongue found me
all but bursting in a big fat raindrop on your lip.
You licked me in and it was, well, exquisite.

Later I lived frozen in a glacier for a hundred years
before melting into a river that flowed past your house
where you went for a drink one day. (I saw your reflection
in the water's mirror.) And there I was again -- inside you.

It's nuts how our hearts keep finding one another
across all time, space and eternity. Because once
you went swimming when I was the ocean
and I felt you and turned warm for you
so you could move around easily inside me.

What ecstasy! You swam so delightfully that day.
We were two spirits dancing on the waves. It was
the perfect moment. But now you're hot. Dirty, too.
And I beg you stifle that laugh. Because this time I'm
gushing out of the faucet as you take your bath.

Thank You For Not Leaving Me

(For Sandy)

Honey, what's with us? Rather than discuss stuff
we disagree on everything. Why, you always take
the other side! If I say left, you say right. If I say day
you say night. Tomato, to-maw-to. Potato, po-taw-to.

You pick the one I choose not. It makes me mad but
you do it anyway because it's part of your Libran DNA.
I've had to learn to accept it that we're always staring
at each other from opposite sides of the Great Divide
between us. I think you just don't want to get caught.

I'm a lark and you're an owl. When I'm cold, you're hot.
When I'm in the mood you're not. Let's face it. You and I
are absolutely, positively no-doubt-about-it incompatible.

Driving together? OMG! Forget about it. You're happy
going slow in the right lane behind a truck. I get apoplectic
and say WTF! I'd be in the left lane trying my luck at racing
ahead of the traffic and being first in line at the next light.

Look, I know I'm not always right. But neither are you, Mrs.
Always-Has-to-Have-The-Last-Word. That's so annoying
by the way. And childish, don't you think? Yet somehow
we get past ourselves and don't pay our grudges forward
nor let cold shoulders stay cold. We find ways to move on.

So even though you're my demon, you're my angel, too.
And even though you throw me into the pit of despair
you also toss me a ladder so I can climb out of there.

I suppose that's fair. What can I say? You're the other half
of my brain and you frequently drive me insane and all but
bat-shit crazy but you're yin to my yang, my wild thang;
my boomerang – the only one who ever came back for me.

You're a seductress and a tyrant, a Caribbean pirate and
a robber baron on my Rhine; the neighborhood burglar
who peeps through my window, the thief in the night
who breaks into my mind. Oh you! My alpha and omega
my beginning and end; my sweet forbidden garden of Zen.

You are my sexy under-cover lover buddy and my best friend.
The Rubik's Cube I couldn't fix; the taste of wine upon my lips.

I know we also clash and bang, but that's part of life and the
mess it brings. On the other hand, we've taught each other
so many things. Come to find out there's worth in those lessons
and as for learning them, I'd rather do that with you. Let's face it:
the chances of someone else 'getting' me are infinitesimal.

So I hold on tight to you and me as we face what life brings:
The tears, the pain and the suffering. And yes, some joy, too.
The tough one for me is living with another human being.
It's hard enough for me to live with me – much less you.

I'm a handful, an emotional roller-coaster who's hard to please.
If love were war you'd have the Iron Cross with oak leaves and
for good measure, we'd toss in some Purple Hearts because
you should get a chest full of medals for living with me.

Sweetheart, remember when we were twenty and first met?
I wrote you these lines when you went home one weekend:

*You came with the force of wind-driven rain, and when you left
I swore I'd never known such pain. When will I see you again?*

That was decades ago. Yet I still feel this way. I love you and can't live
without you. So even though I give you reasons each day to fly out the
door and never look back, thank you for not leaving me.

Cats And Wives

My cat loves me but swipes with razor claws
so people say I should give him away because
he sometimes hooks one in me. It's scary,
granted, and painful to watch a thin line of red
open up along my arm or leg. You rat for a cat!
Once again you've done your master harm.

But those same people who say give him away
don't see him rubbing my shins at four a.m. when
my feet hit the floor and here comes Buddy Boy
with steady tread and oh so happy to see me again.

Then he sits on my chest purring and splaying
two white paws with ten sharp claws that gently
knead my breast, each claw a pinprick hinting
at a veiled threat of pain and more bloodshed.

Instead, I delight in watching him purring and
loving and kneading me. And sure, that little rascal
with a pink nose and white toes melts my butter
when he stares me straight in the eyes and says:
You trust me not to rip your heart out, don't you?
And I, thinking of consequences, gulp and say yes!

Wise men say the truth hurts and love sets us free.
I ponder this as my cat sits idly on me purring and
kneading me, loving me and smiting me just as you,
wife, sit idly on my heart, purring and needing me,
loving me and smiting me, pinpricking with your claws
whispering: *You trust me not to rip your heart out
don't you?* And once again I gulp and say yes!

Eckhart Tolle says he's known a few Zen masters,
all of them cats. I think my kitten, whom I found
trembling and starving under a car, isn't into Zen.
He favors claws, paws and mice -- not meditation.

And you my dear? You're an enigma, a riddle.
I know little about cats. Even less about women.

I'm All Yours Today

Honey, I'm sorry about yesterday.
Truly sorry. That was a bad day.
I couldn't stop blowing up. You,
the world, politics – everything.

Please forgive me. I'm all yours today.
I'll do anything you say. Seriously,
you are my sweetie pie. If it came to you
or getting high, I'd choose you. Please.
Don't laugh. That's a big thing for me.

So yes, anything. If you want to go shopping,
I'll walk down every aisle with you. Slowly.
I can't believe I said that. I hate shopping,
which you do constantly. We could even pop

into the fabric store while we're out.
You already know how I feel about that.
But I'll go because I don't want to lose you.

And when we get home if you want to explain
the bills slowly so I'll understand, I promise
to listen. (Man, I can't stand the bills.) But
I don't want to lose you. So just tell me
what you want and I'll do it for you.
But can we set a limit? Say, six tonight?

Love, What's With You?

Love, I asked you to come at me
in all your glory and help me write
an awesome story equal to Lara
and Yuri in Doctor Zhivago or better
yet: fair Romeo and Juliet. Instead,
you sent me Cupid who fluttered in
with a pointed dart and a wicked fart.

Now that's no way to treat a poet
who rises each morning at three
to sail the stormy seas of human need
and emotion, charting a hard course
with only his words to guide him.

I was looking for hope, joy and inspiration.
And frankly, they couldn't come too soon.
Alas, all that happened was I had to open
the window and let some air into the room.

You're Just A Heathen In My Temple Of Love

Sweetheart, what's with you? You've changed.
I once fancied you as some kind of cute little lamb
or maybe a vestal virgin of sorts with a big bosom
and a long white gown -- sorta see-through -- and
your entire aura topped with a golden crown.

I don't know. Maybe I was asking for too much
letting my expectations get the best of me.

Be that as it may I tried to stay in the game
when I lit that candle of exotic scent – jasmine
and sweet tea – and you said you couldn't see
a bloody thing and turned the light back on.

At which point I would have been delighted to see
a black velvet chemise or sexy teddy come floating
to bed, but instead your hair's all pinned up and
by God, you've got your old rumpled jammies on!

I had my hopes set so high that you would stride in
wearing heels and those red silk stockings that go
all the way up to your thighs. That's why I sighed when
you flopped in wearing your bunny rabbit slippers
over old gym socks and I was looking for a sexy fox.

Vowing not to be dissuaded, I played a tantra mix
of sensual, pulsing music with dancing ladies and
you said *What is that?* like you just ate something bad.

I replied that you should try to broaden your horizons
why don't you please? Then went to light some incense
and – I should have guessed – it only made you sneeze.

I said *Gesundheit!* and *I hope you don't catch a cold.*
You said *Just a minute, honey* and put me on hold
so you could check the weather on your phone.

Lord have mercy and bless me from above! Woman,
you're just a heathen in the temple of my love.

I Don't Know Where My Poems Come From

I'd be hard-put to explain
where my poems come from.

I think most of them are about
things I run from. And while
that's true I know where I want
them headed: to your heart, where
I hope they become imbedded.

Why? Because a poem contains a truth
if the poet gets it right. A poem, then,
is a wonderful thing that sheds light.

Now, most folks aren't ready for the blaze.
Bright light scares them, makes them afraid
of what they might see. But say, friend,

don't you know that's the only way
to get your spirit healed? You have to follow
light and truth to get to something real.

If you have another way I'm anxious to know it.
Because I've tried all the booze and dope
but they're simply not as good as a poet.

You Lead With Peaches, But That's Not All

Your name is *Chele*-lektu and so I must ask:
What the heck have you been up to? I see
that you lead with peaches. That reminds
me of a joke about sunny beaches. Yet

You're Ethiopian and grow in Yirgacheffe.
I imagine it all crazy with giraffe necks
and berries hanging from coffee bushes;
berries that, when roasted, taste delicious.

Admirably, you've got more than peaches
to brag. You fill the bag with notes of lemon
and raspberries and lots of chocolate on top.

Truly, your flavor are quite remarkable.
I love to watch you sparkle in the cup
eagerly waiting for me to drink you up.

Inhaling your sweet aroma wafting in the air
is an aromatic delight beyond compare.
Chelelektu, when you and I begin the day
I get a good feeling things will go my way.

So here's to coffee growers in Chelelektu.
I wish you the best; that's what I hope for you.
And those beans you grow? What a cup they brew!

This Wretched Poem

I don't like this poem!
It's going way too deep.
Finding all kinds of things
I don't want to keep.
Opening doors I need
to shut. Good God!
What is this stuff?

It's dark. It's death.
It's Satan's breath and
sex with a witch's hex.
Everything I've wrecked.
Oedipus Rex. Mother,
Father, all the thoughts
I've always avoided.

It's lovers and liars,
haters and fighters,
cheaters and deceivers,
losers and leavers.

I hate this poem. It's a little
shit-digger and dredger-upper
of dirty deeds, dark thoughts
masturbation and way too much
chafing consternation along with
plenty of world-class agitation.

This one's going way too deep.
Going for all the marbles I want
to keep hidden: my sins, things
that can't be forgiven. Oh yes.

This poem's bringing tears
to my eyes along with the loss
of everything I hold sacred.
Its got me stripped down
cold and bare-ass naked.

Damn! What's that saying?
*"Be careful what you wish for.
You just might find it."*

How true! I wanted a poem.
Now it's beating me black
and blue and I'm trying
to run out of this hole
because this poem's out
of control. It's snapping
drill bits, bursting hoses
collapsing tunnels and
devouring miners whole.

Then it's headed for me
to grind up my soul.

It's a killer poem.
That's all there is to it.
I don't want to get
anywhere near it.

Yet here I am, pen in hand.
Staring at the damn thing.
Keeping that drill bit spinning.

Raising Poems

Poems, I tried with all my might to raise you right.
I built you up and pushed you along, then smiled
with pleasure as you grew big and strong. I made you
the best I could. Now, even though my pride in you
wells in my breast, I need to nudge you from the nest.

You must find a place in the world to call your own.
A place in the world where you can sing your song.

Some of you lucky few get to inspire. That's a fun job
for a poem to do. Yours is the spark that starts the fire,
the torch that burns so hotly bright, igniting love's desire.

Others of you sing of freedom. You must find it. And when
you do, ring liberty's bell loud and clear. Never let doubt
or fear slow you in that purpose or interrupt it. You poems
are blessed with glory. Yours is not to die. Get up there

on the rampart with your flag. Wave it high. Your voices
contain freedom's cry. Come, my friends, my poems --
meet me at the barricades. Be the song on our lips as we
fight the rich who stole our dear country away from us.

You can do it. I made you this way. Go forth with your spears.
Stab evil in its black heart. Do your part to raise mankind.
This is what I had in mind when I blew breath into your lungs
and opened your eyes. Roar then, like the lions you are.

Many of you must find hearts broken, blue or cracked.
Your task is to mend them. Be glue to glass, mortar to brick,
solder to tin. Stop pain. Put people back together again.

Use your keys. If they don't work, remember the correct
combinations that spring open the locks binding chains
tight around victims trapped in misery and sadness.

Yes -- emancipate sad people from their despondency!
Above all things, you must do this for me. Stop suicides.
Freeze fingers on gun triggers, hands on neck ropes.

Make stomachs throw up the dope people swallow
in the hope they'll never wake again. Give these
poor folks and tortured souls a future to believe in.

I know that's heavy lifting, but this is the work I built
you to do. I'm confident in your competence to save lives.

Besides, remember the promise we made when I created
you guys? You said you wouldn't be wooden Pinocchios
without souls. You are poems, thoughts and clever words
carefully crafted to play major roles. I command you: go do it.

All of you are noble. All of you are true. You are my best beats;
the strongest lub-dubs from this heart of mine; the loves of
my life. But now you must fly. Go with God, my children.

Do what you have to do. And never forget that I, your Father
Creator who made you and grew you, will always love you.

A River Of Stars

(For Matthew)

Long ago when the grass was green
I paddled us down a winding stream
where mossy branches hung so low
and the current carried us to and fro.

I stopped at an island to beach the boat.
We jumped out on the sandy bank
and devoured our snack of potato chips
and peanut butter-and-jelly sandwiches
we later said was the best feast ever.

You got jelly on your lip. I said *I'll get it*
and licked it off. This led of course to
passionate kisses. My love, what bliss
it was to be alone with you on an island
in a lazy stream on a summer afternoon.

I poured cheap wine into paper cups
looked you in your eyes and toasted
our love, then talked about how lucky
we were to have found each other.

You took a sip of the wine and said
you didn't need it, that you were all
full of love for me, and that was enough.

You laughed and said *Who needs wine when
I have you?* And remember the warm drops
of rain that fell? We grabbed the blanket
and pulled the canoe over us and by God —
didn't we make passionate love?

You held me tight and whispered fiercely
with your breath hot upon my neck *I don't want
to ever let go of you, or for this moment to ever end.*

And I said *Of course it won't, you silly goose.*
Haven't I already told you our love is forever?

But as we know the way it goes, summer breezes
turn to autumn leaves and lazy streams freeze
hard over. In winter we grabbed jackets and
stood outside shivering as we watched the stars
wheel past overhead at night, and we said:

One day we'll be up there with them shining
bright for the ones we love, and for each other.
Then we'd run back inside and jump in bed and
hold hands or make love until sleep covered us.

And the stars kept burning and Earth kept turning.
Spring came, water thawed and the old canoe
banged restlessly against the dock, anxious to
be out with its bow in fresh water. But I got sick.

And once again you held me tight and said:
I don't want you to go, or for this moment to end.
But spirit had already made that decision
even though we didn't understand the reason.

My love, did you know that Achernar is an island
in a river of stars called Eridanus? It's quiet and
mysterious and it's going to be delirious
to drift with you down that lazy stream in heaven.

Instead of branches hanging low it has comets
that glow and stars named Akari and Zaurak and
Acamar with the absolute best beaches you ever saw.

That's where I'm waiting for you in the old canoe
to paddle us out to the moon. I've made us a snack
so when we come back we can enjoy our feast on

our heavenly beach, and you can once again look
at me and say: *I hope this moment never ends.*

And I'll laugh and call you a silly goose again.
And remind you that it won't because I promised
our love would go on forever and ever. So rather
than go back inside and get in bed, we'll hold hands
take a big ol' jump, and get up into heaven together.

We'll be two stars then, shining bright -- shining for
the ones we love and shining, always, for each other.

What Would I Do Without You?

What would I do without you who always has my back
my front and sides? Let's just call it: you have all of me.
Belly to brisket, head to toes, that is how our river flows.

So thank you because I can't always hold myself. Sometimes
I run through my fingers like water and puddle-up on the floor.

Now there's a helpless feeling for you. Other times I'm fire;
I burn things down. No, that's not the size of it. I'm volcanic,
atomic. My explosive temper flattens shit, levels trees and
leaves mushroom clouds behind as validations of a kind
testifying to the work I do that destroys everything in my view.

Then, when nothing's left, when only ashes blow and sweep
across the burning prairie, you're still standing next to me.

You don't call me an idiot. You shove a hammer in my hand
and toss a bag of nails at me and demand that I get busy.
(By the way: I hate it when you do that.) But you don't leave.

For reasons I can't comprehend, you stay. So thank you
with all my heart for that. The exact words to express
my gratitude at the size of your sacrifice simply don't exist.

So what would I do without you? Oh that's easy. I'd be dead
and buried long ago under a cross at the end of a row next
to a one-lane cemetery road cars creep on all day, keeping
me from a good rest, which I never got while alive, either.

So thank you in advance for saving me from all that eternal
insomnia after I'm dead. And here is where I'd like to remind
you: I wanted to be cremated anyway, Honey. Remember?

Saturday Morning Couples At The Market

You can always tell which couples made love,
had sex, did each other or whatever. They walk
hand-in-hand, rubbing and nuzzling like horses.

Those who didn't are downcast. He strides ahead
of her. She, knowing dawdling angers him, dawdles
over nothings, increasing the increasing tension.

Two couples, but only one blessed. One in purgatory,
the other in heaven happy with seraphim. Behind them
comes the sad couple, grinding on the same old story.

My Cat

Gosh darn it! Here we go again.
It's four a.m. and I want to pray
but my cat's not having any of that
today. Food – that's what he craves.

I get a tin, pop the lid and yuck.
It's that stinky stuff I can't stand.
Ocean whitefish and tuna pate.
My little guy thinks it's grand.

He gobbles it down and smacks his lips.
This makes me think I can sit with Jesus
but my cat wants more of that awful crap
that smells so bad I keep it in the fridge.

So I get up and give him some more of it
to which he turns up his little pink nose.
You see, the problem is that it's cold.
Five seconds in the microwave does the trick.

Now the air smells like someone took a
you-know-what, but my cat's happy
wolfing down his rancid seafood feast
to which, by God, I have to hold my nose.

I've been told that dogs have masters
while cats have servants and I, too, must
confess to being burdened with a feline pest.
In fact, he's purring right now on my chest.

Do Lions Eat Poets?

The Lions want more poems this morning.
They're roaring at my door. Fellas, please.
I implore. It's four a.m. They don't care.
They demand I write again even though
I wrote last night until ten. They're cats.

They're nocturnal and don't mind if I'm tired
and unable to wake. *Get up! Get up!* they cry.
You've got new poems to make for us!

It's no surprise to surmise a lion likes a steak.
But who would know they also favor poetry
on the plate? Those rascals even pick their teeth
with Chaucer, Yeats and Pugh when through.

And since I am one of the three I must work
my poems so diligently for these kings of beasts
who move from verse to meat so indiscriminately.

They're really rather insistent. They set deadlines
and I dare not miss them because the threat's
implied that if I do I might end up inside them!

Listen, Poem – You Have To Go

You overstayed your welcome at least a week or two
even though I told you our love affair was through.
Yet still you keep bringing me back to you. M*on Dieu*!
ma Cherie. It's well past time we bid *adieu.*

You must get over yourself. I have so many more poems
that gather dust on the shelf waiting to be done. So scat.
Scram and adios. At this point we're only chasing ghosts.

Can't you just finally admit we're through? I remember
patiently reviewing your rhymes so many times I was
losing my mind and going blind. And your meter? Please!
Bless Matthew, Mark and Saint Peter. Your iambs, dactyls
and spondees truly had me on my knees. I'm in a bad way.

My needle keeps skipping and jumping in place on your track
each time you circle the record player and come on back. Truly
I'm not grooving to your beat anymore, but when I try writing
new poems, you return and I get stuck on your scratch again!

So I took my record player to the trash bin and I tossed it in. I
said: *Goodbye friend, who needs you*? And oh how my heart flew
that night when I got a new poem just right in my head and took it
to bed with me, its voice a lullaby singing me to sleep. But when
I woke at dawn I discovered you'd smothered it dead. Its memory
was gone; my words and ideas for it flown. And I'll be damned.

I began working on you again! So now you know why you must go.
You've gone from being a busted record with a broken track to a
hungry boa constrictor trying to make a snack of my poems when as
a matter of fact it never could be, would be or was all about you.

The Junkie Poet

When I was a junkie and shot heroin
I always looked for a vein to stick it in.

First things first I'd be up at six jonesing
like a mofo for my fix, eager as my needle
to be sucking at the sugar on my spoon.

I'd grab my kit, get my shit, cut it in lines
on my mirror but not roll no dolla bill.

Oh hell no. I tied my arm off with a rubber hose
and poked a needle in to draw a drop of blood
into the syringe to ensure I was in the vein before
I pushed the plunger and shoved the drug in.

Oh yes. I rode the Main Line. Heroin? Cocaine?
Ecstasy? All of them worked for me. I went down
paths I shouldn't have tread. I hit rock bottom
and gave myself up for dead, was a white sheet
and a living corpse riding on a wild China horse.

But the universe turned and somehow I endured.
Did my higher power keep me here to give me words?
Because I'm not shoving heroin through a syringe
anymore. I'm pushing ink through a fountain pen.

And sure, I still chop up lines, but I try and get them
to rhyme in iambic pentameter. And I still get high
but instead of shooting up coke or speed or horse
I'm shooting up words. I know that sounds absurd.

It's funny and ironic and uplifting and sublime that I'm
still riding the Main Line, only with a pen this time.
You know, people ask me if it hurt to poke a needle in
my arm and I reply: Not so much. Try writing a poem!

The only way I can explain it to you is like this:
Junkies like to shoot their dope; poets crave words.
So, poetry or shooting dope? There's no difference.

Things Made Of Glass Sometimes Break

I offered you my heart with love and said *Please
take care of it for heaven's sake.* But I guess I forgot
to tell you: Things made of glass sometimes break.

Why, just last week you went to give it back and I said:
Honey, wait a second. Look at this – a great big crack!

You replied: *Don't worry. Remember Leonard Cohen?
You like him. He said cracks are how the light gets in.
Does that thought somehow make you feel better now?*

Uh, no – not really. The shape you returned my heart in
leaves me reeling. I recall you said you'd guard it with all
of your love and vigilance, along with lots of diligence.

Yet, I sought my heart in your apartment but it wasn't there.
You said: *Don't worry silly boy. It's in the basement.* So,
down I went and no it wasn't. Here's a wild guess, you dirty
rotten miscreant: you hocked my heart to pay your rent!

You know, it's hard to be happy with a cracked heart.
Yet when I told you I thought you broke it you said:

*Remember Gene O'Neill, your favorite playwright?
He said man is born broken and lives by mending. Thus,
that crack in your heart means you can begin healing now.
You can thank me anytime. Isn't all of it just splendid?*

Uh, no, I replied. *I don't think it's splendid. I'm hurt.
Neither do I feel like mending at the minute.*

And you said: *Darling, remember Humpty Dumpty
with the great fall? They fixed him, so we can get
your heart back together again in no time at all.*

Oh is that right? You think my heart's like a village in
Vietnam that must be destroyed to be made whole again?
That's not much of a game plan. Besides, you got that egg story
dead wrong. All the king's horses and all the king's men could
NOT put Humpty back together again. Geez. Where you been?

And then you say: *Oh pu-leeze. You can be such a drama queen!*
I'm no female alien grey who popped in from the Milky Way.
Nor am I a space chic from the Mother Ship. I'm just trying to fix
our relationship before it takes another dip in that toxic pool
of argument where our tempers flare and burn us up quick.

Nothing wrong, I respond, *with that. But if we can focus please*
on my heart all busted front-to-back. And you say *Don't worry. I*
know a guy blows glass. He can get his torch right on that crack.
Now gosh darn it, woman. A torch on my crack just won't pass!

Darling, you say, *Look at it this way. It doesn't matter if your heart*
shatters. I have Super Glue, Gorilla Glue and Monkey Glue too -- lots
of apes to fix those fractures in your glass heart.

Apes my ass! You can keep your glue and your goofy attitude
on all things emotional and tender. When it comes to my heart
I'm not into "Return to Sender." Got that, you shatter cat?

I didn't drop your heart on purpose! I'm just a clumsy person!

You're a quack is what you are. I don't know why I stopped by
your sugar shack with my heart of glass. I should have flown
to Mongolia and ridden a yak or traipsed to Africa on a giraffe.

Could I even do that? With my luck, they'd pitch me off and I'd hit the
ground, certain again to crack my great glass heart.

The Argument

Honey, you know I try and tone it down for you
but that at the end of the day I'm just a guy
through and through, so I'm thinking hips, thighs
legs and breasts. Can't we just get undressed?

I think it's really urgent that we do because I find
new life in you and the words we used this morning
only threw up yellow caution lights of warning.

Now, I love words as much as anyone else but
sometimes folks has got to shut their mouths
because there comes a time when words don't do.

I'd say we're there. It's time to take our clothes off
and simply let our bodies talk. After all, you and I
are going through life together, a stallion and a mare
attached to the same tether. And at this moment

I think our bodies could do much better than our brains
and mouths have done. What trouble they've caused!
Talk, talk and talk some more. Seriously, we've explored
all the topics. Let's take a vacation to the sexual tropics!

Honey, we both know a man needs sex to get to intimacy
and a woman needs intimacy to get to sex. So let's not labor
under a voodoo hex. Hips, thighs, legs, breast. Can't we
just get undressed? How about if I volunteer to go first?

Miss Muhondo, The Coffee Bean Flirt

Miss Muhondo, you remind me of a certain girl
I never caught in high school. I chased her
just like I'm chasing you all over Coffee Town
into one espresso bar after another, vainly
trying to nail your flavors down because
at the end of the day I'm such a coffee clown.

Now, every time I taste your cup I spy you out
the window running up Arabica Boulevard and I,
liking your red grape and marshmallow, follow.

But when I catch you at two-hundred degrees
you intriguingly taste like tart cherries to me.

Then, cooling down to one-eighty-five, you arrive
at cranberries, which is amazing, leaving me
wondering about magic in the cup. You flirt, you
Coffee Town runaround. I get a hint of one of
your tastes then you lead me on another chase.

Once you and I went down a buttery slope of caramel
which was like, wow, how did you do that? Some even
say its chocolate and honey you sport, while others
declare pear makes you pert. Miss *Muhondo,* all I know
is you change flavors as often as you change your skirt!

And you do this in Rwanda, you little coquette. You know,
it may take me a while, but I'll nail your flavors down yet.

Pie And Poetry

My wife has a mind of her own.
I'm telling you that right now.

Anytime she's inclined to agree
with me she gets a furrowed look
on her brow and her brain says
Don't do it! No way, no how.

The fact of the matter is
we're incompatible and
she can't agree with me
on a blessed thing. No sir.
That's not the way she rolls.

I tell you, she's contrary and
fundamentally predisposed
to turn a friend into a foe.

Sometimes it gets so bad
I pack my bag and say *adios
muchachos* and sorry, but
we're not even getting close
to love like Romeo and Juliet.
And honestly, it makes me fret.

And she says: *You know what?
I've been thinking of making a pie.
What kind might you like?*

Now, I like many things in this life.
One of my most favorite is pie.
Bake me one and cut me a slice
and yum, yum. I'm all yours.
And guess what? No one makes
a better pie than my lovely wife.

So I set my bag down by the door
and say, *Oh I don't know. How about
blueberry or cherry?* And she says: *Sure.*

I've been married forty years and love
my wife in many ways but never more
than when she makes me a pie.

So she bakes me one with loving intent
and I breathe content and decide to stay.

I was raised in an angry house and got
whupped up good with a leather belt
when I was a kid for things I never did.

Fury then, is in my veins and all my life
I've tried to restrain anger surging in me.
But that's a battle I don't always win.

And honestly, sometimes I feel so bad
at how I've struck out at my wife I can't
sleep at night. So I get up at four and write
a poem about how I love her and won't ever
be so angry like that again. But it's too late.

The next morning hers is the bag packed and
she's the one saying *I can't handle us.
Our love's been hijacked by a band of thugs.*

And I say: *I understand. But please read this
before you leave.* And hand her a poem I wrote
called "Thank You For Not Leaving Me" plus
one titled "What Would I Do Without You?"

She reads them and I watch a tear roll slowly
down her cheek. And she looks at me and says
Really? And I nod my head and say *I'm so sorry.*

You know, people always ask me what makes
my marriage so breezy and I just smile and say
that one's easy. The answer is pie and poetry.

Kainamui Coffee From Kenya

Kain-a-mui, I love your name-a-mui because
it rhymes with Ooey Gooey but I don't think
you're related since Ooey's a worm all soft
and slimy with a dull, flat color and you're a bean
all hard and shiny with a bright black sheen.

Anyway, I'm just saying your name makes me smile
and even though you're not a camel I'll still walk
a mile for you who are full of ruby red grapefruit
pineapple and cherry candy which my taste buds
think are just fine and dandy, sometimes better
than even candy, which gives me cavities; or liquor,
which is quicker but makes me sicker in the morning.

So there's no shame in my game to say that my mouth
wakes up yearning to taste you and get at you and that
my eyes delight at the sight of you sparkling in my white
porcelain cup. Meanwhile, without a smile, my poor tongue
slobbers drool like a hound-dog fool straining on a chain and
oh so eager to be slurping and licking coffee from your bowl.

Seriously, Kainamui, if I can't get to you I'll be out of control.
Scalded? My taste buds tell me: *Take the chance!* Even now
they stand in line for the honor of a step or two in a waltz
with you and say a slight scald would be well worth the dance.
Kainamui, I even dreamed of you last night. My God!
the scent of your aroma. Sorrowfully, my glee was dashed
when I woke without you and discovered I was in a coma.

My sheets were soaked, the pillows were on the floor and
I was desperately needing more of your grapefruit, pineapple
and cherry candy. Why? It's five in the morning – I've got to get
going! I trust you'll set my nerves a-jitter and jolt my laggard
brain a-twitter. Welcome, then, my dear sweet Kenyan friend.
With trembling fingers I lift the cup and – ah! -- drink you in.

Sex Slave

My wife's funny. She can't see things in front of her face.
For example, yesterday we looked at apartments and --
I'll be damned! The manager wanted us to move in to use me
as a sex slave to pay off the rent! When I mentioned this to
my wife she said I was getting carried away in my head and that
no girl in her right mind would ever want to go with me to bed.

Now see? For the sake of marital harmony I have to let things
like that go. But when we stopped at the store on the way home
the cashier kept gazing at me and wanted to jump my bones.

I turned to show this to my wife, but she was on her phone.
So I told her how lucky she was to have landed a catch like me
when the fact is that all the girls want to play patty-cake with me.
She said: *That's nice sweetie. Do we need more cottage cheese?*

It even happened telepathically on the way home when my eyes
met a blonde's at a stop light and she let me know she'd do me in a
New York minute. I mentioned this to my wife and she said: *That's
nice, Honey. By the way. Do you have any thoughts on dinner?*

She says these sex fantasies are all in my mind, but I believe she
must be half-blind not to see all the ways women throw themselves
at me. I guess I emit a special glow when I walk down the street.

I didn't know this gift was bestowed on me. It didn't come all at
once. I grew into it slowly. But my silly wife can't see any of these
things. She thinks I'm inventing legions of lusty, panting women.

And I want to say: *That's it exactly! And furthermore
they want to use me for a sex slave.* But I know that one
will land dead as a corpse and cold on her porch so I
keep my counsel to myself, of course. But women!

I have no idea what they're all about. And beginning
with my wife, there's no way I will ever figure them out.

Lion And Turtle

Lion caught a story idea.
He chased it down
wrestled it to the ground
and now (smacking his lips)
enjoys the taste of it.

Turtle (state of shock)
finally catches up.

Good God, Lion! What have
you done and how do you
account for this awful mess?

You're wallowing in grisly
sentences and I see ripped-up
adverbs splattered across
your furry chest. Not only that,

but a bruised relative clause
drips from your bloody jaws
and pieces of noun meat hang
from your wickedly sharp claws.

And it's hard to believe but I
think I see participles dangling
from your ginormous fangs.

Dang, Lion. You've also split
an infinitive in two, along with
a big mess of predicate adjectives
and a dreadful confusion of the
pronouns "whose" and "whom."

I'm actually not sure I have a
broom so big and pens enough
to clean up your writing mess.

*I'm watching you gnaw through
a whole slew of mixed metaphors
and suck clichés from bone marrow.*

*It's all pretty well-known that
this is no way to write a poem.
You gruesome beast. I hope you
enjoy your gory feast. As for me,
it's nothing I would want to eat.*

Lion chews pronouns off a leg,
tears indirect objects off a hunk
of breast, then snaps a branch off
a nearby tree to pick out pieces
of grammar caught in his teeth.

He spits out bits of fat and gristle
along with mixed metaphors and
one of Alexander Pope's epistles
to Doctor Arbuthnot (and other
literary what-nots). Then he lowers

his great Leonine eyes, bores a hole
straight through Turtle's hard hide
and lets out a mighty lion ROAR!

*Are you kidding me? When it comes
to this manuscript, I created it. I'm not
the cleanup crew. That's for you to do.*

*As king of beasts I only chase the feast,
then eat the meat. The rest? The editing
and straightening, the tidying up, all that
dictionary and thesaurus work, too?
That's all on you, dear reptilian friend.*

Remember our roles: I, writer and Lion,
create the buffet. You, Turtle and editor,
clean it up. It's therefore plain to see
that's not my drink in the cup: it's yours.

Now get busy. Convert this heap of words
into priceless treasure beautiful and true
that gives maidens reasons to sigh for and
lads causes they think they need to die for.

I hope that's not asking too much of you.

Turtle (mucho mas exasperation and
no small amount of indignation) snaps:

Very well you bloody beast! Once again
you've laid a hacked-up mess of words
at my feet. Now I, with stern resolve,

leathery paws and a great literary heart,
depart, only to return tomorrow morn
with a brilliant piece of writing art.

Lion, I'm not sure you understand.
I, Turtle, am vegetarian. And you?

Not to be contrarian, but you are
most decidedly a full-on carnivore,
a wild and raging writing barbarian.

My Barnyard Cat

(For Ian and Melissa)

People saw you as just another cat
but Vader, you were so much more
than that to me. Jet black and off
an Iowa farm, you had a twinkle
in your eye that said I'm so excited
to be your new best friend for life!
Can we go to my new home now?

And you were the best cat ever.
Your purr was as big as your heart.
You got it started and couldn't stop.
Lap cat? You sure were. And always
so happy to see me walk in the door.

You counted on me for goody treats and
I took such joy at indulging you in feasts,
then seeing you curl up at my feet. Vader,
you gave me so much love for a cat.
I'll always be grateful to you for that.

And I loved you back. You know how much
I didn't want you to leave but I thank you for
finding me and being at my side the morning
you died. Jeez, little guy. That was so hard.

I held you as a kitten when you were new.
And I held you when your life was through.
And all the time in between, I prized all the
sweet love you shared with Melissa and me.

You were our ornery boy, a counter-climber
who brought us such joy. So take care buddy!
I'll see you again in heaven. You were so much
more than just a cat. You were my best friend.

Red Lion Amaryllis

Red Lion led the bloom.
She came charging out.
First to grace the room
she was gone all too soon.

You too came charging out.
You graced my life. You filled
my room and left too soon.

Seasons come and seasons go
just as summer sun turns
to winter snow and then
spring shows her face again
with new flowers growing.

But none like you, Red Lion, who
graced my life and left too soon.

Modern Poetry

I tried reading modern poetry.
And I got lost. I didn't know
what they were talking about.

So I asked a poet how come
they carry on that way and
he said they all wrote like that
nowadays. Stretching words,
loosening lines. Not bothering
to make a rhythm or a rhyme.

I thought about that a hot minute,
Told myself to keep an open mind.
No harm in trying. So here I go.
I'm reading a modern poem . . .

Hmm. What is this? A broom is
pumping blood; the moon is singing
and misery limps along on a crutch.

C'mon, man. Isn't that a bit much?
Did you ever see misery limping
on a crutch? Not me. Look, I'm just a
simple guy willing to give poetry a try,
but poets have got to make sense
if people are going to read them.

Where else can we get laughter, wit
and wisdom along with inspiration?

I never went to college nor do I consider
myself full of knowledge. I just like poetry.
So I'm confused as to why modern poets
feel a need to play brain-games with me.

I grew up on Dickinson, Plath, Thoreau
Poe and Philip Freneau who wrote
about a bee drowning in a glass of wine.

Now that's my kind of poetry. As for all
this modern stuff – I don't know what
to call it. A bag of mishmash mixed with
some balderdash? How about fruit salad
or jambalaya? Not sure what to tell you.

A woman asked me the other day about
modern poetry and all of its weird ways.
And in truth, I didn't know what to say.

I couldn't help her, couldn't guide her
through the maze. But she had children,
so I told her to keep their minds clean
and free. And to get them as far away
as she possibly could from modern poets
peddling their nonsense and insanity.

For they gather up a big wad of words,
rear back and heave them at a wall.
Then say a prayer and hope like heck
that some meaning emerges from it all.

Oh What Coffee!

This coffee's pushing all my buttons.
Even ones my wife can't find. I said:
Hey coffee. Those aren't yours.
They're hers! Coffee replied:

Oh shush. Stop pretending you mind
my flavors sublime that wrap around
your tongue and entwine your taste buds.
Your wife's a wife. I'm Coffee. We're best
kept separate. You know why, don't you?

I, confused that I was talking to Coffee,
lacked a meaningful reply. So Coffee
spelled it all out rather simply for me.

Do you think she'd understand how crazy
you are about me? Because if she did
she'd throw a hissy fit and cut you off.
See why we should keep your coffee lust
a deeply held secret just between us?

After I picked myself up off the floor
(again, because I was talking to Coffee)
I agreed with Coffee and, relieved, lifted
the pot and poured myself another cup.

Have You Seen My Brain Today?

Pardon me, Friend, I hate to ask you because
I'm from Nebraska and a wee bit bashful
But: Have you seen my brain today?

Because last night it climbed out the window
To play with Dish and Spoon and later a plowboy
Said he saw it with the Cow jumping over the Moon
While a cat scratched a fiddle for to play a tune.

You see, Uranus -- planet of insanity -- really got
Her hands on me. Then Moon who rules all water
Emotions and tides showed up and damn!
Those two crazies took me on a wild ride.

I woke up naked and cold from breezes
My face all covered in green cheeses.
The jailer barked: *What did you do*?
I said: *Sorry man, I haven't a clue.*

I then looked out the window of my cell
And threw the Moon a great big yell.
What's going on? I angrily demanded.
Yet Moon just hung in space and grinned.

So Friend, you see how Dish, Spoon, Moon and Insanity
Somehow got the best of me because I'm still trying
To find my brain and that stupid cow. And is it me
Or do you hear somewhere a little dog laughing?

Silliness and moon cheese; beeswax and bumble bees.
People crawling on their knees; don't ask me what it means.
They're just silly scenes in poetry. But seriously. If you see
My brain today -- that dear old gray old matter that helps me stay
alive – give me a shout, won't you, Friend?
I'd be much obliged.

Marriage SOS

Honey, I'm really sorry about last night.
I didn't mean to get us in another fight.

You need someone who doesn't do that
to you and I need someone who will do me.
So please . . . tell me why we're still married.

What happened to our relationship!? Are we
sinking sailors who should have left the ship
a long time long ago and now face drowning?

Is this it, then? The dreaded end? Or do we jump
cling to a spar, holler out and hope for rescue?

A Poem I Wrote Is So Mad At Me

I told this poem when it was coming through
that it would heal the rift between me and you.
So I gave thanks and was happy with the work.

I created a character, plus a point of view. Wrote
and rewrote the words and lines so many times
before finally getting them to rhyme and ring true.
I buffed and polished so hard my rag wore through.

I put so much love in the poem I wrote for you
all in the hope it would help bring you home.
I opened my heart for it, which wasn't easy to do.

Then you visited. I showed you the poem and
what madness was it that you gave my words
a cursory review before tossing them aside
and all but sneering: *What small fry*. That's right.
You wouldn't read the poem I wrote for you.

That's why this poem is mad at me. He says I'm no
Socrates, that I write words that just don't please.

He says I didn't make him as big as he could be.
That he wasn't built grand enough and with all
the right stuff to finish the chore I aimed him for;
namely, to reconnect with you, the love I once knew.

I thought I built him strong enough but no – he's
pouting and quite displeased. He says he wanted
to be Hercules, Achilles or some other Greek hero
who could at least slay a mythological beast or two.

Instead, this poem's exasperated. Says I'm over-rated.
That I've failed as a coach and now he wants traded.

The Distance Between Stars

They say it's a long way from Earth to Mars
but I've got one for you: How about the distance
from my heart to yours? That's a measure
oh so far; that's the distance from star to star.

Not Moon to Saturn, nor Neptune to Mercury;
rather, Hercules to Taurus or the Southern Cross.

Once the planets were so much closer; so too,
were the stars. Then you went super nova, felling
them like tenpins into Scorpio's bloody claws
and blasting the remnants out into cosmic fog.

Now my telescope won't bring you who once shone
so brightly into view. I gave up hope, packed the scope,
smoked a cigarette and threw the butt to the wind.
I get it. You moved on to the other side of something –
a cold dead planet in a distant galaxy, I suppose.

That's a distance oh so far. That's the distance from
star to star; the distance from my heart to yours.

I would set out to regain you but I don't have the faith
you'd come and fetch me if I got stranded in outer space.
If I dangled by my lifeline and hung by my wrists would you
look at me from inside your cozy capsule and think:
Hell no I'm not going out there. He's not worth the risk!

Really? Has it come to this? I'm a rescue mission you can't
commit to? Because if my suit got ripped my skin would freeze
and my bones would shatter all down to my knees. And this:

Before I could say your name a final time, forces in space
would rip it from my lips and tear it from my mind. In fact,
I'd have less than a minute to live. But that may not bother
you because, come to think of it, that's how it was when
you visited. So what's the difference -- you, or dying in space?

I Wish To Be A Bad Poet

They say the greater the pain the greater the poet
and that's certainly true, I suppose. Those folks,
after all, take volumes of prose and convert them
into poetry all focused and flowing, that deals with
thoughts heavy and dark like prophets with omens.

If you consider the price the good poets paid to find
their rhymes and meaning, you'll discover something
downright alarming. They were out with the hounds
more than a few bricks shy of a full load, had bats
in their belfries or didn't have both oars in the water.

And ultimately, all that looking into the deep hole
of the human soul lead to their deaths by suicide.

Don't believe me? Let's take a look at Vachel Lindsay.
The way he writes about time being a loom spinning
illusions will stop you in your tracks. I don't know why
he drank a bunch of lye but it sure ate his guts out.

Gee, Vachel. That's no way to die. Like you swallowed
a bellyful of rattlers and they started biting you inside.

Then there's Sara Teasdale and Sylvia Plath, favorites
of mine who stuck their heads in ovens and turned on
the gas. Reading them I found my kindred spirits, but
it was plain to see their pain in life was too exquisite
to make their time on Earth more than a brief visit.
Yet it hurt me so to know they felt they had to go.

Living in Nebraska, I favor regional poets. That's why
I like Weldon Kees from down the road in Beatrice.
He wrote a novel, poems, played jazz piano, painted
and one day jumped off the Golden Gate Bridge.

Weldon even once wrote a poem about cats, as did I.
So we're brothers in more ways than one because
he was creative and like me thought of suicide.

And did you know Oklahoma gave us John Berryman?
God blessed this man and cursed him I guess because
I kid you not he was a straight-up train wreck alcoholic
with four ex-wives who nonetheless won the Pulitzer Prize
then jumped the Washington Avenue Bridge in Minneapolis.

Over in Iowa, Tom Disch wrote great fiction and poetry,
then ate a bullet in nineteen sixty-eight after predicting
America would one day be filled with inequality and hate.

I'm sorry, Tom. Your words came true. So it's probably
best you checked out early, not late, rather than watch
the horror show in the USA unfold as man reverted to ape.

So I wish with all my might my Muses won't alight and
help me pack my lines tight with lots of metaphors and
hidden meanings. In short, I need to be a bad poet.

I need to struggle to get rhyme and rhythm right
in order that I might drive across a bridge without
having the urge to park my car and go jump off it.

Oh I know I should quit this writing business. I should just
stop trying. I'm into life and living – not poetry and dying.

The Author

I got me a writing machine. It's lean and mean
and fast and clean. Turns itself on each morning
at four, sits on my desk with a purr, purr, purr
all kitty-cat idling, disguising the fact that it's a
Wildcat Four-Forty-Five that roars out onto the
writing highway gobbling blank pages up alive.

And oh it's nice that my writing machine's so light
to the touch. I don't have to push it much, intuitive
as it is and knowing automatically what to do for me.
Its pistons explode in my mind as I race against time
frantically trying to write down so many new lines.

Sometimes it even helps me drive because I'm dashing
with such ardent desire to yet another writing fire.
Hairpin turn up ahead? No sweat. I'll blow through it
at ninety-five burning rubber and screeching the tires.
I can't be slowing down with my head so full of ideas.

My machine comes with chrome wheels and fat tires
red racing stripes down the sides, bumpin' tunes and
plush attire plus a five-speed power shifter on the floor.
What a delight, and such fun it is with eight cylinders
and so many horses for my brain to ride. The rear end?
Jacked-up, friend. Mufflers? Throaty, growl like beasts.

I get my machine out on the literary freeway at my desk
with miles of paragraphs to burn. I pop the clutch and
squeal the tires, hope you stay out of my way because
it's a sunny day and I looked around but didn't see
no cops around so I took the top down and stomped
the gas pedal all the way to the floorboard metal.

When I hit a hundred miles an hour, that's when I hear
the po-lease sirens. Highway patrols and state troopers
sure can be some party poopers, but can they catch me?

Because I'm slamming gears and bashing fenders like
a crazy drunk on an all-night bender. Bumper cars?
We play that, too. You hit me, I hit you. I'm no angel
neither are you and we ain't singing in a heavenly choir
so I'll knock you off the road to be first across the wire.

Not many drivers get too near me. I try and keep them
in my rearview mirror. Most broke down or crashed
in the dirt. I tell you, writing is a dangerous sport.

My machine loves me dearly and would never steer me
into a collision or catastrophe, nor leave me with an
over-heated writer's block. That notion's pure poppycock!
People say: *Really? You got a writing machine gives you
that much?* I laugh and reply: That's right, you chumps!

Then I get 'er back to town, act all proper, slow 'er down.
Oops -- here's the mayor. Look sharp and throw a wave.
Good Day, Sir! Here's to you and how's the Missus?
And I hope you're happy with our municipal business.

Nighttime comes, the writing's done and my machine
cools off on my desk, resting and purring for me, eager
to be out again as I sleep, dreaming of tomorrow's ride.

Git On, Boy. You Ain't No Poet

Really? You're a poet? That's a good one. Hardy har har.
Best thing I've heard today by far. C'mere Boy, I'll tell you
something true. Gather close. I won't mince words with you.

If you haven't been dumped by a true love, fired or abused,
cursed at, made fun of, come in last or got unjustly accused
you're never gonna make it as a poet. I hate to be the one
to tell you it's not going to happen: no way, no how, no sir.

I know you went to college and got a poetry degree, supposedly
learning about iambs and troches, metric feet and beats; images,
irony, alliteration and those extended metaphors called conceits.

Yet I glance at your stanzas and see no such structure undergirding
your poems. I get forensic, dig deeper, inspect your poetic bones
and discover they're all broken and cracked. What's with that,
Jack Sprat? Why can't you put down whose and whom alongside
doom and gloom, or rhyme boo with hoo, you silly goose?

We're waiting for you to do that. I also saw your class attendance
showing you weren't only a skipper, but when assignments came
due you turned them in late and just by your knickers. So you're a
pretender, a hack; a joker bluffing his way through a hand of
academic poker; a scribbler, someone who is at best mediocre.

In fact, we still laugh at your brain blast last semester when you
took alliteration under debate, then moved on to Burns, Shelley and
Yeats, a task you said turned your head into a crater filled with jelly.

Look. See that farmer cutting wheat in the field? He's the poet
because he connects with something real, framing his days
around mother earth. That's great poetry of sorts -- growing food
from the ground; feeling good at sundown after a hard day's work.

You know that poem "Trees" by Joyce Kilmer? The farmer thinks
about it when he drives his tractor under the row of oaks alongside
his field. He hears nature's song. Feels the wind in his face and the
breeze on his skin. Sees the sky overhead. This is what makes him
a poet, not you who deep-dove into lying and conniving, boozing
and bed-hopping, snorting coke and smoking too much dope.

Look, when the farmer was in the barn all night pulling a calf out
into the world you were playing games with girls you wanted to
seduce; passing out drunk at daybreak, waking up at two o'clock in
the afternoon. Good Lord. You're a mess! What happened to you?

And when the farmer toiled in the rain all soaking wet, you cruised
the internet looking for porn. When he got his hay all put up
in the barn, you were trying to encircle girls with your filthy arms.

It's like this: You have to be able to see and hear and feel and care
about things. Perhaps if you ever learn how to be real maybe you
can write a verse or two. Until then, good luck being you. We'll all
be sure and take a side-step when we see you coming through.

So get this figured out; then and only then can you come back and
talk about what it means to write a poem. Until then, just git on
with yourself. And take off your sunglasses, your black cowboy shirt
and your black jeans and boots; plus the ring that goes through your
nose. Do us all a great big favor, would you? Drop the act.

And change your major. Maybe to history, marketing or math.
Because one thing's for sure -- you sure as hell ain't no poet!

The Dying Fall

We slew the dragons at the gate
defending the castle of our love.
Then filled the moat and sank
their boats coming after us.

We bore the cross and kept the faith.
Threw a buck on the collection plate.
Prayed to Christ with all our might.
Resisted evil as it slithered in the night.

We courted and wed. Visited our sick
and buried our dead. Said goodbye
to mom and dad. Lost all we ever had.

We grew old together, intertwined.
Let each other into our minds.
Put on suits and fancy dresses.
Climbed our ladders of successes.

We rolled the dice and won it all.
Drank too much alcohol. Bound
our wounds and bore the pain.
We drove each other insane.

We danced along the primrose path.
Spent German marks and French francs
then turned around and broke the bank.

We dug the hole then paid the toll
when we couldn't get out of it. We fell
back down and said "Oh shit!"

We shot the moon, drove home late and
left too soon. We tried once, then twice
but still lost the toss. We cried hard tears
and died inside; held on until our fingers
bled. Slept in late on a feathered bed.
Discovered sex under a quilted spread.

 We tempted Satan, painted the town red
went to jail and threw each other's bail.
Played the games our egos demanded
and somehow came up empty-handed.

Got stoked, smoked dope. Partied late.
Gave up hope. Sang the blues. Flew
the coop, paid our dues and then lost
everything when fate clipped our wings.

Shared food when there was barely none.
Had a daughter, then a son. Scrimped.
Pinched pennies. Dreamed together.
Chased rainbows. Worked hard.
Danced, sang. Fought and made up.

My love, it's true we had some bad days
and problems were aplenty. But all the
same you broke my mind when you said this
time we were at the end of the line and you
were finally going to leave me. Really?

Finding Myself By Getting Lost In You

Sweetheart, I just read that Neptune is a giant ball of
methane gas and if a person stood on it they'd sink in
up to their chins, then drop all the way into the center
of the cool and icy-blue planet. This made me laugh
because you are so cool and icy blue just like Neptune.

So I decided to soften your mind by flying to Neptune
and standing on you to see if I can merge with you.
That's right. I'm headed your way in outer space since
we're no good divided. United. That's the ticket.

When separated, we don't work. We're discordant.
Our parts get all out of order. That's why it's important
we line our chakras up and burn some kundalini while
merging our auras with the universal and cosmic energy.

It's true I'm hot through and through and therefore
a stranger to your icy blue. But I'm also wise enough
to know you complete me and I complete you. See?
Merging, that's the thing to do. Uniting in symmetry
like yin and yang and ebony and ivory on piano keys.

Don't you agree? Look, I'm the giver, you're the receiver.
I'm the river; you're the river bed just as I'm the wedding
but you're the feast and I'm the seed but you're the one
who gives birth. Get it? I'm the house but you're the hearth.
You're the dove; I'm the beast. You are Shakti, I am Shiva.

I push down and you pull up. You are anima, I am animus.
We're angel dust and heavenly gold, opposite sides of
the same story always told throughout the ages. Your soul
seeks mine and mine seeks yours. You are my missing piece.
Without you I'm incomplete, a book without its pages.

Seriously, have you considered we could be prototypical
Adams and Eves? Because it's true I'm a tree, but without
your fruit my knowledge is useless. And I'm a battery but
I need you to convert me into electrical energy just as
I need you to be my best, for without you I cannot manifest.

This is why we've got to blend our hearts and minds like
the two snakes of DNA climbing up the caduceus, oh you
Great Mother, you Gaia and Yemaya, source of all water
and mistress of creation without whom I am useless.

So I'm flying out to Neptune to merge with you and sink in.
I'll find myself then as I descend, savoring every minute of
losing myself in you. My burning hot with your icy blue.
Oh what sweet synthesis! The most perfect blend I can
imagine will be finding myself by getting lost in you.

I'm In Poetry Jail

Wife come to visit me in the county jail. Said:
Hang tight Honey. That judge done gave you
holy Hell but I'm raising money to throw your bail.

Next day I'm in front of him. He says: Sunny Jim
you in a heap of trouble now. You done went out
and committed a felony by writing some poetry.
I won't ask you how you plead for writing them.
The look on your face indicates you're guilty as sin.

You're a malcontent, one of those ink-stained wretches
who's always bitching and kvetching about the way
things are. You're against the status quo. Well, I'm here
to let you know if you don't stop writing those poems
I'm going to give you a room of your own in a luxury suite
at the state pen. Comprende? Verstehen? Understand?

I said Si and Ja and yes I do! Then promised him
I'd burn my paper and toss my pen; so he put me
on probation, but not without this admonition:
Don't you write no more of those poems again!

How can I explain this drive that compels me to write
poetry in order to feel alive? I can't breathe without
verse. I feel dead inside when I can't paint with words.

So I did my best to bend my mind to all the ways
of humankind. I read books on math and physics.
Took exams in computer programming. Watched
more TV so I could join conversations around me.

I went north and west and east and south. I went left
and right and was super nice to everyone I met. I kept
my eyes open and my mouth shut. And yet, for all of that,
the truth I stuffed down so deep inside still came out.

And each time I reached for paper and pen my wife slapped
my hand and said: *Honey, you don't understand the mess
you're in. Judge said don't write a poem again. You've got
a nasty habit of telling the truth, as your poems attest to
but all that honesty just causes the authorities to arrest you.*

But I couldn't live in the world of money-money and
spend-spend-spend and always having to contend with
me first always and screw you anyways; and thus withdrew
again to the corners in my mind with pen and paper to see
what I could find and wouldn't you know it? It was a poem!

When the judge saw what I wrote about him he got all red
in the face and threw my ass in the state pen for a solid ten.
He brought the gavel down. He told me I was a clown and a
complete disgrace. That being said, he added: *I'll set you free
when you make up your mind to stop writing that damn poetry.*

Pluto And Persephone

He had all the right props: slick chariot
big black horse. Scare the hell out of you.
But hey, you know: Pluto. That's what he does.

A theatre major, dramatic lad lusting for
Persephone who, once she got over the shock
of seeing him rear up from the ground
and abduct her, saw how he longed for her
with such passion and would never hurt her.

So she had to consider: Wasn't it incredible
to be wanted like this? Overwhelming, really.

Don't Eat Those Pomegranates, Persephone

There was the bargain
all backed up that
if you drank his wine
you'd stay in the cup.
So you went thirsty.

And when the food
came whistling through
you gritted your teeth
and said "That won't do."
And you went hungry.

Then he told you his story
about a family squabble
that all went bad, and
you wondered about that.

He called your name
in sleep at night and at
daylight brought flowers
all of which made you lose
track of the hours.

Now wasn't it strange
how it all ended up?
You drank his wine
and stayed in his cup.
Ate his food at his side.

Persephone, Persephone,
with your pomegranate seeds.
Twining hearts, mending needs.
When you realized how much
Pluto cared, you stayed.

Don't Ever Write A Poem

Don't ever write a poem. Just don't do it.
No one would read it. Not your mother
your brother, your father or your lover.

Your words would be too real, make them
squirm and wonder what got in to you
that you thought you could write a poem.

So don't do it. Save yourself a lot of grief.
Try tennis or golf. Go jogging. Blow coke.
Hit some bars, get drunk or smoke weed
for relief. Surely there's enough pain in
your life you don't have to write poetry.

I found out the hard way one day when
I wrote a poem about a fighter pilot
who died while bombing North Vietnam
which is what my father did, except that
he didn't get shot down: he came home.

In the poem, however, I killed him off.
That was my bad. Dad said: *Jesus Christ
Craig! Aren't I going to die soon enough
that you have to kill me off in a poem?*

Why he took it so seriously is still a mystery
to me. Jeez, Dad. Where's your objectivity?

I also wrote a poem for Aurelia, the front-end
manager at the Mercado where I used to shop.
She dyed her hair purple and pink and made me
laugh. When I saw her I would say: *Buenos Dias,
Aurelia! And what color is your hair today?*

That's the name of the poem I wrote for her
but she hasn't talked to me since then, which
is why I say don't ever write a poem. Get up.
Get out. Do something away from home.
For the love of God, just don't write a poem.

Once an old girlfriend from high school told me
that her mother and she thought I was weird
and that it figured I wrote poetry. Jeez! Sadly
I think that's the way Aurelia feels about me.

I've been known to tear up easily. Perhaps
my sensitivity scares them away from me.
Or do I dredge up unpleasant memories?
Why, they act like I work in a mortuary!

Then there's Sheila down the street whom
my wife and I were glad to meet last year
and get to know. So back and forth we'd go
with goodies, cakes and casseroles, feasting
as much on each other's company as we did
the delicacies we'd baked for each other.

And yes – I ended up writing her a poem
about love and friendship and generosity.

But she had a dog. A really bad dog who
lunged and barked and nipped and bit.
And Sheila was so protective. Instead of
controlling it she let the dog run wild.
On me. Lunging and barking and nipping
while I would be trying to sip some wine.

And then one night I was trying to read
the poem and that damn dog wouldn't
leave me alone. When it nipped at me
and broke the flesh, I got up and left.

So Sheila's dog ran me out of her house
but she says I provoked him. Get it? It was
my fault the dog bit me that night.
(Maybe the dog just doesn't like poetry.)

Did she call me later and apologize? Sure.
Dream on, star gazer. I tell you. It's a crime
and a sin to get treated this way by family
and friends, all because I write them poems.

So don't ever write a poem. Doing so will bring
more grief and gloom down on you than you can
conceive. Plus, you'll wake up way too early and be
out swimming with the stars and chasing the moon.

If I Were A Woman

I got a poem that's driving me crazy.
If I were a woman and it was my baby
I'd sue the hospital, the doctor and
the medical school she went to, and also
the flesh on the bones in my body for
creating this mess of poetry inside me.

The lines came out breech, bringing no mirth.
No little girls. No bouncing baby boys. Just
difficult birth. Meter that broke me down.
Rhyme schemes that tore and wore me out.

I'm throwing in the towel, crying poetic foul.
On my way to file a complaint with God
and the Muses, too, for creating this mess
of ideas inside me that I grew. I pushed so hard.
And then to have them come out this way!

There's just no doubt about it that I would be so
ape-shit nuts and out-of-my-mind bat-shit crazy
if I were a woman and this poem was my baby.

I'd put it on restriction the minute it came out
for all those times it kicked me in the gut and
punched me in the snout. That little brat.

My Poems

Some of them are big.
Some of them are small.
Some have lots of meaning
Others not much at all.

But they're all mine.
Each and every one.
Some like daughters.
Some like sons.

They pinched and prodded.
They poked me and hurt.
Some I choked on. Others
put me face-down in dirt.

I wrassled 'em and I boxed 'em.
And boy, they sure hit me back.
Some I was able to leave behind.
Others just kept coming back.

One or two broke my heart.
Another took out my mind.
Three or four tore me apart.

One in particular was vehicular
causing a pileup deep in my soul.
It took weeks to get whole again.

Heroin addicts love their smack.
It's sugar on their spoon. Me?
I'm addicted to a Goddamn poem.

The Cat And I

The cat and I are crying this morning at 4 a.m.
He says meow, I let him out. Meow again
I let him in. Meow, meow, meow, he cries.

I'm not my cat, nor can I see through his eyes
but I know he cries for his mother whom I found
dead down in the old creek bed behind the house.

That's why I cuddled him and brought him in.
He's my little brat, my wild rescue-kitten.

I cry for my mother, too, now that she has died
because I never knew her when she was alive.

So the cat and I are crying this morning at 4 a.m.
He says meow, I let him out. Meow again, I let him in.
Meow, meow, meow, he cries for a mother he has
never known while I sit in the dark writing this poem.

The Break Up

It's going to take a long time getting over you.
I'll do all the things the broken-hearted do:
Take long walks in the park, watch late-night TV
in the dark. Play sad songs about love and loss.

Mornings I won't have anyone to bring coffee to
or salute with a cheerful: *Hi Honey! How are you?*

So I'll try and spend more time in creativity where
with any luck I'll forget all those things you said
about you and me. I'll work extra hard to stay inside
my poetry, swear to God I'll get more writing done.

I'll find new activities so I won't feel so all alone,
things to do that keep me too busy to think about
us together at home and the way things used to be.

I'll ponder all the games we played: the this-for-that
the tit-for-tat, all those "got-you-backs" as I drink beer
and watch the cat sit where you once sat. I'll look at
pictures of you and sigh and take them down after a
few years go by to stop your eyes from burning mine.

You once said I was a treasure to be admired but
that sentiment must of come with a pop-up timer
because you told me you were tired and that our
relationship had expired. Okay I guess. If you insist.

And yet, I must admit I understand how it came to this.
When I spoke my truth you called me a liar, and when I
lit my flame you ran in and tried to put me out.

Tonight I'm thinking of the future and what it may bring
without you being part of anything. Five years from now,
maybe ten – why, you could be dead by then. The fact is
I won't know when things happen to you because you got
all in a big huff and said you'd never talk to me again.

You're a good person; I am too. So how in the heck did
we make each other so blue? I don't know. We just did.

You said you loved me, and I replied: *I love you too until
the day I die!* But that didn't matter when we gathered at
the rim of the hole where our love had been and discovered
we could never fill it back up again. I'm sorry, kid. That was
a bitter pill: the realization we'd reached our journey's end.

I'd tell you how much I miss you but I live in an empty space
of grief not so prone to speak like in those good-ol' days.
I'm actually struck quite dumb, if not a bit numb, by events
as I ponder the fact that there's no longer a you and a me.

Growing Poets

You think orchids are hard to grow?
Some folks pick up a poet. Ever try
one of those? You take them home
only to wish later you'd picked up
a rose or maybe a couple marigolds.

So I'll tell you in case you're not aware
of all the love you'll need -- and care --
to pour in a poet if you want to grow it.

First off, those rascals often catch a cold.
So you'll be making hot toddies and tea
and wondering why you didn't get hostas
snap dragons, poppies or some nice lilies
instead of picking up a scraggly old poet.

Try a clematis. They're less dramatic than
a poet. And also less likely to come up with
mold, mites, blight and mildew right under
your nose before you know it. And of course

poets are well-known for finding it difficult
to separate from Mother Plant. Sometimes
they don't root very well without her nearby
clinging as they do to her apron strings and
finding it hard to thrive without her loving gaze.

And don't look to Daddy Vine for praise. He lost
his mind a long time ago in a series of wild and
raging rants when fire ants crawled up his stalk.

He got on the insecticide then, to get away from
them, but now runs up and down the squash and
tomato rows, then turns around and goes out

on all-night benders with the weeds! Of course,
some of the poet-plants take up his wild ways.

So I'd balk if I were you before I took a poet home.
Maybe walk around the parking lot, think it over.

After all, they're known to have so many maladies.
Make sure you dust their leaves. And don't forget
to set them out so they can get plenty of fresh air
and breeze. Even so, they'll still fall over and skin
their knees. You'll have to pick them up then and
offer lots of love, encouragement and sheltering.

So keep my tips in mind the next time you think
you might take a poet home. They can be grown.
It's not impossible. But they're like a lot of things:
You just need to know what you got ahold of.

Cat Lovers Visit The Dog Park

First, full disclosure: we're cat lovers here
on reconnaissance and bear you no ill intent.
However, what we see is rather alarming.

A bunch of dogs running around like
they've lost their minds after eating
some hallucinogenic mushrooms.

It's difficult knowing what to make
of such commotion. And then the way
they're sniffing each other's behinds.
Don't you find that somewhat offensive?

And how about the way they shamelessly
squat in front of you and take a big shit?
That's something no self-respecting cat
ever did. Dogs – those idiots – don't think
nothing of it. Why, they don't even cover it!

And as for running around, a cat only runs after
a rat; otherwise the word that follows cat is nap.
And cats don't bark. You'd never know a cat was
in the room unless you heard a modest meow.

Plus, cats are nocturnal. They creep and slink
in the dark. They don't run around like fools
in a park with their tongues hanging out and
drool slobbering off. Cats, being felines, act
with dignity, not savagery like canine beasts.

And is it me? I don't mean to be indelicate
but don't dogs smell a lot? Good God!
It's too much for our noses, which is why
we won't be copping no reposes in this
dog park because all these silly creatures
are barking their heads off. We're leaving.

Sooner, not later. And we'll run, not walk
to the gate; and not, like Sarah with Lott
in Sodom and Gomorrah look back on that
smelly old dog park where all we hear is
bark-bark-bark and the truth of the matter
is we'd like to hear some purrs – not pants.

So we're off post haste to hit home base and
chill out on our couch with our cats on our laps.

Senior Center Poetry Class

Jambo! Jean. And what's new, Stu? Susan
good to see you as always. We're poetry geeks
who meet once a week at the Intercultural
Senior Center on Center Street, seeking a
verse or two in order to make sense of things.

You could say we get centered in The Center.
We put our troubles aside to spend an hour
inside a circle of light in a well-lit room
where we take delights in flights of poetry.

It's actually quite a treat, if nothing else
for all the people you meet. Jean has come
a long way from The Congo, Rwanda and
a refugee camp. She's a survivor, a woman
of great strength, grace and dignity. With her
I stumble around and try to speak Swahili.

I think Stu's a good ol' boy like me who tries
not to get too far ahead of his skis. I like that
and sure hope he knocks out that poem about
Nebraska football games he went to as a kid.
I'm glad I can be here to help him write it.

Susan's from New England and has a mind like
a steel trap. Just last week in class she recited
a poem about some frogs in the sand who got
run over by a dune buggy on Martha's Vineyard.
It was a funny poem and I wish you were there.

So for sure: The Senior Center's a place where
the four of us meet to twist up words in the air.

And even though four may not sound like much
to you, Emily Dickinson said it only takes a clover
and a bee to start a prairie -- and reverie. So now
you see how we four can grow our own poems.

I'm the reverie. Stu? I believe he's the clover
while Susan and Jean I think are the bees.

But I have to tell you something about those three
that's funny and ironic to the supreme. They think
I'm teaching them, but they're the ones teaching me.

They're teaching me about faith and persistence
about hanging on and not giving up. And that's why I go
each week. I talk with Stu and Sue and Jean, and together
we try and find a little art in life by talking about some poetry.

Poetry Infestation

Bugs was running everywhere.
I heard them under the stairs
in the garage and out in the yard.
Some was even in the parking lot.

Scurry, scamper, scuttle, scoot.
My discomfort was acute 'cause
them little critters was all about.
All them bugs in all their hordes
was driving me out of my gourd.

Orkin man come over; Terminex,
too. I said: *Hey Fellas. What the heck.*
Bugs turned my house into a wreck.
Could you therefore please inspect?
I got run over by a bunch of insects.
My floorboards sag. Ceiling, too.
Now I'm crazy as a freaking loon.

Bug men said they'd see what
they could do. They prodded
and peered, looked and poked.
Even got out their microscopes.

But what they saw through the lens
dashed my hope for peace again
when they looked at me and said.

Sir: we're honor-bound to give you
our best advice; so here it is. It's not
fire ants, roaches, fleas, tics, termites
or mice you got. It's even worse.
You're infected with poetry and verse.

I knew then that I was whupped.
I grabbed my chest, found a bucket
and kicked it because any fool knows
if you go against the laws of the universe
by writing poetry and verse, the prognosis
is always fatal. That's what you get if you
go out and try and rock the cosmic cradle.

I Want You To Be Happy

Cards fell hard between you and me and
I'm sorry I was a big part of your misery.

So, if my absence brings you peace, fine.
I'll help enforce your banishment decree
and ensure you won't see me because,
believe it or not, I want you to be happy.

If thoughts of me being lonely and suffering
give you joy, great. I'll keep walking the street.
If thoughts of me being sad fill you with glee
I'll keep being sad if my pain makes you glad.

I seek a routine now to keep me busy.
Buy groceries, mow the yard; walk the dog
get the trash bin to the curb on Thursdays.
I'm at home, I'm at work. I'm in traffic looking
at a wreck. Thoughts of you hang everywhere.

The sun comes up, the sun goes down. I get up.
Pray in the dark. Walk around getting older and
feeling your heart grow colder. The Pleiades rise
now in the east through the branches of the tree.

It's all the same to me. Neither does Aldebaran
call to me nor break through my wall of apathy.
To it all I act indifferently while walking out alone
searching for meaning now that you're gone.

And oh how the wind blows through me.
And the water, too, flows through me.
I'm hollow as a shell and not coping well.

I lie awake at night wondering what I did that
caused you to leave; but the answer eludes me.
All I know is that you can't stand to live with me.

This of course puts me out on the street alone and
sad, enforcing your banishment decree because
at the end of the day, I just want you to be happy.

I Got A Deal For You

I know you got hurt through and through
and someone deeply wounded you. I get it.
You're defensive, lash out and act mad.
I understand. I've had anger, too. Still do.

But since I'm not the one who cut you and
I've been cut too, how about this? If you
don't bleed on me, I won't bleed on you.

Blood's best kept inside us where it does
bodies most good. It only spouts and makes
a mess, causing problems when it leaks out.

We both know life's a game of chance with
winners and losers, and we're a pair of dice
thrown by drunken gods playing the odds.
We hit the table hoping for snake eyes
and bust out when the toss turns otherwise.

We're survivors, then, you and I who try
and keep our faces to the sun. Clutching faith
and what's left of broken hearts and loves
we hold on, praying for moments of grace.

Obviously we both need rest and healing.
And since I'm the one in front of you maybe
you can rest with me and I can rest with you.

But first, how about if we make this for a deal?
If you don't bleed on me, I won't bleed on you.

The Weary Poet

The poems are banging on my door.
They're strewn across the table
and scattered about the floor.

Some slither up from the cracks.
Others crawl under the carpet.
Everywhere I look I see more
and more of those damn poems.

Everything's a verse to me. People
strike me emotionally. Easily hurt,
I process the grief by writing poems.

Now they're boiling over in the pot.
They're whistling madly in the kettle.
They're mashing down my gas pedal
making me an urgent demon-devil.

They're blasting me down the highway
at a hundred miles an hour. Lord, Lord.
They have so much horsepower their
pressure's about to burst my tires.

Indeed, these poems are the flames
roaring in my fire. They are the truth in
my aim and the bore-worms in my brain
giving me thoughts I can't say or explain.

There's no doubt about it. They're testing
me and my grit. Asking me if I've got
the talent to be a poet and if so, prove it.
I'm not sure anymore. I'm worn down
to the bone and had about enough of
these damn poems. Now, if only they
would go away and leave me alone.

About The Author

I can't remember a time when I wasn't reading poetry, and that goes
back to being a little boy. I've always written poems, too. Like my mind, I
suppose, they range from the silly to the sublime, the cosmic to the
comedic, and the tragic to the absurd.

That said, here are the jobs I've held to make a living in this life.

Editor, 6940th Security Wing base newspaper. Goodfellow AFB, San
Angelo, Texas.

Staff Writer, Airman Magazine. Kelly AFB, San Antonio, Texas.

Editor, Air Combat Command News Service. Langley AFB, Va.

City Hall Reporter, The Longview (Texas) News-Journal.

English and Writing Instructor, The University of Nebraska at Omaha;
Metropolitan Community College; Iowa Western Community College.

I didn't volunteer to be a poet and neither do I
choose my poems. All these words were put
in my mind from emotions deep and unknown.

One day fate tapped me on the shoulder and said
Craig, how come you're not writing a poem? Me?
I don't know. Is that what you want me to do?